IN AND OUT
THE SHADOWS

IN AND OU

HE SHADOWS

Poems by **Sandy Brownjohn**

OXFORD
UNIVERSITY PRESS

Illustrated by Oliver Gaiger

OXFORD
UNIVERSITY PRESS

Great Clarendon Street, Oxford OX2 6DP

Oxford University Press is a department of the University of Oxford.
It furthers the University's objective of excellence in research, scholarship,
and education by publishing worldwide in

Oxford New York

Athens Auckland Bangkok Bogotá Buenos Aires Calcutta
Cape Town Chennai Dar es Salaam Delhi Florence Hong Kong Istanbul
Karachi Kuala Lumpur Madrid Melbourne Mexico City Mumbai
Nairobi Paris São Paulo Singapore Taipei Tokyo Toronto Warsaw

with associated companies in Berlin Ibadan

Oxford is a registered trade mark of Oxford University Press
in the UK and in certain other countries

Text copyright © Sandy Brownjohn 2000

The moral rights of the author have been asserted

First published 2000

British Library Cataloguing in Publication Data available

ISBN 0-19-276246-X

1 3 5 7 9 10 8 6 4 2

Typeset by Danny McBride Design

Printed in China

For A. C. B.

Contents

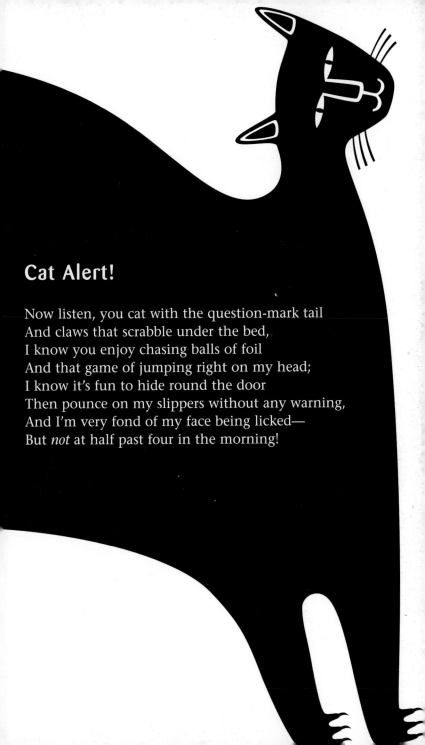

Cat Alert!

Now listen, you cat with the question-mark tail
And claws that scrabble under the bed,
I know you enjoy chasing balls of foil
And that game of jumping right on my head;
I know it's fun to hide round the door
Then pounce on my slippers without any warning,
And I'm very fond of my face being licked—
But *not* at half past four in the morning!

Beware of the Sheep!

Chorus: Beware of the sheep! Beware of the sheep!
          Don't try counting them when you can't
          sleep!

One sheep, two sheep, three sheep, four
Won't jump over the gate any more.
They dance the tango, roll on the floor,
Bang on the drums and climb up the door.

(*Chorus*)

Two sheep, three sheep, four sheep, five,
Every one of them is on the skive.
Show them a gate and they'll contrive
To backflip, somersault, or take a dive.

(*Chorus*)

Three sheep, four sheep, five sheep, six,
Please jump the gate, now, no more tricks.
Don't stick your tongues out! Fiddlesticks!
All sheep are born mavericks.

(*Chorus*)

Five sheep, six sheep, seven sheep, eight,
They hop, they surf, they ski, they skate,
They jump on each other after lying in wait,
But they won't jump over that pesky gate.

(*Chorus*)

Six sheep, seven sheep, eight sheep, nine,
If only they would stand in line,
Instead of knocking back the wine
And linking arms singing 'Auld Lang Syne'.

(*Chorus*)

Seven sheep, eight sheep, nine sheep, ten,
Let's just try it once again.
W-a-i-t for it! I'll say 'when',
You miserable ovine specimen!

Beware of the sheep! Beware of the sheep!
Count something else if you want to go to sleep!

Exercising Demons

Deep in the centre of the burning earth,
Old Nick surveyed, without any mirth,
His demons' ever-expanding girth.
He said:
The living round here's too free and easy.
I can't have imps with stomachs like that!
You lazy devils, you may *well* look queasy—
By Lucifer, you're fat!

For greedy imps who overeat
There'll be hell to pay if they can't compete—
In the battle for souls, the race is to the fleet.
I want:
Every one of you to do PE,
Graft till you wish you'd never been born.
By Lucifer, each day there'll be
Aerobics at dawn!

You'll get the full diabolical works
With a daily dose of physical jerks,
And woe betide any little devil who shirks!
For you:
There's no escape from the dread treadmill
Or the scrabble up the sides of the bottomless pit.
You'll work out your penance for ever until
By Lucifer, you're fit!

Potshot

Have you got a terracotta pot, or what?
I've got to have a pot for the spot on my whatnot.
I forgot that a whatnot ought to have a pot
And a terracotta pot would hit the spot.

Great Scott! I had a lotta terracotta, yes a lot,
But I've got no terracotta pots now, not a jot,
For the upshot is I got shot of the lot.
So, what about a pot with a forget-me-not?

A forget-me-not! A forget-me-not!
And not in terracotta but an ordinary pot!
I wanted terracotta and you offer me this rot!
You can keep your rotten, misbegotten,
    pettifogging pot!

Raining Cats and Dogs

Dogs cock their legs at trees, at posts, at walls,
Or anywhere they please,
Oblivious of disease.
Dogs are liabilities.

But cats dig holes to pee, (and turn their backs
To gain some privacy),
Then bury it completely.
Cats show sensitivity.

All to Blame

Oh, I am a mink, and a very fine mink,
I'm a very fine mink indeed;
But I won't end up with the other minks
All draped round the shoulders of greed;
For I am a mink that is on the loose—
I kill and I eat and I breed.

Yes, I am a mink that is on the loose,
I am a mink who's been freed.
I make my own way in the world
And follow where freedom will lead.
I take my chances with the guns
As I kill and I eat and I breed.

Oh, I take my chances with the guns
Though many a mink will bleed;
There's more than one way to make a killing,
And killing is my creed.
It takes one killer to know another—
Me? I kill and I eat and I breed.

Yes, it takes one killer to know another
And keep them up to speed.
All freedoms have a price to pay—
You reap where you've sown your seed.
Whether profit or protest, I'm out in the cold,
So I kill and I eat and I breed.

The Strange Boy

I know a boy, he's a very strange boy,
When all is done and said;
Though his head's screwed on, his face doesn't fit.
He has eyes in the back of his head.

He can sometimes be all fingers and thumbs,
All eyes, all ears as well; he
Has a finger in every pie
And his eyes are bigger than his belly.

The cat's got his tongue, there's a frog in his throat,
And butterflies in his tum;
When he cut off his nose to spite his face
He stuck out like a very sore thumb.

He was born with two left feet of clay
And water on the knee;
With fire in his belly and his head in the air
He's elementary.

But sometimes he's all mouth and trousers,
Flying by the seat of his pants;
With woolly-headed, cloth-eared, silken-tongued
Sartorial elegance.

If you threaten to have his guts for garters
He jumps right out of his skin;
He has no stomach for his heart's in his mouth,
He can't take it on the chin.

His mum thinks he's so good the sun
Shines out of his Khyber Pass;
But right off the top of my head I'd say
He's the strangest boy in the class.

The Loft-Rat

It came in during the summer
when the nights were still warm.
Like a shadowy pirate
it climbed the builders' gangplank
to the space above our heads
to which we gave no thought.

The swifts were still here,
swooping their arcs
into the perfect entry under the pantiles;
fewer this year—
and we didn't see their leaving.
What kept it going may have been them,
after the builders had gone
and all exits were closed.

It came in again, during the winter
when the nights had turned cold,
as a bad smell.
It seeped through the cracks
to the space inside our heads
where we thought of nothing else
but that something had died.

Rung by rung up the ladder,
through the trapdoor,
we fumbled the dark with torchlight
till the body was found
almost camouflaged on the wadding.

The dead rat was still whole
though it stank of rotting forests.
We threw it away wrapped in plastic bags
but the house feels suddenly old.

Catnap in the Catnip
(after Kenneth Grahame)

Down among the catmint
By the garden wall,
Cats are a-sniffing,
Up tails all.

Black cats, white cats,
Ginger cats and tabby;
Fat cats, slight cats,
The skinny and the flabby.

Long cats, sleek cats,
Tortoiseshell and brindly;
Strong cats, weak cats,
The sturdy and the spindly.

House cats, mouse cats,
Pouncers and catchers;
Lost cats, cross cats,
The howlers and the scratchers.

Stray cats, fighting cats,
Every common moggy;
Day cats, night cats,
The fluffy and the soggy.

Street cats, fleet cats,
In and out the shadows;
Tree cats, free cats,
Hunting in the meadows.

Rich, bitch, kitsch cats,
Catty cats and spiteful;
Tough, gruff, rough cats,
Ratty cats and biteful.

Bold cats, young cats,
Stirrers and yowlers;
Old and highly-strung cats,
The purrers and the growlers.

Round cats, straight cats,
Every tiny kitten;
Grossly overweight cats,
The bruisers and flea-bitten.

They're sniffing at the catmint
By the garden wall;
Tranced cataleptic,
Up tails all.

On Being Woken at an Early Hour

The English are slaves to a rhythm
Which doesn't suit everyone—
Just look at the Spanish,
At noon they all vanish
To rest through the afternoon sun.
But the English have work to be done.

There is plenty of time in the morning
For getting through work sensibly.
After lunch the poor English
Slide downhill and languish
And sit around waiting for tea,
For there's work to be done, don't you see.

I'd much rather work in the evening
And rest in the afternoon.
Though it may not be cricket
To pull up the wicket
And declare the innings too soon,
I work best by the light of the moon.

But while we are stuck with this system
My candle must burn at each end;
But I give this plain warning,
Phone at eight in the morning
And I cannot begin to pretend
That you'll ever be counted a friend.

I think days shouldn't start until ten.
Then we all need to have a small break
With an afternoon rest, a
Recharging siesta.
Till that happens, the point I must make
Is—don't phone till I'm properly awake!

Roll Play

Two stoats chasing down a country lane
Threading over and under each other;
Chestnut fur in a twisted skein,
Flashes of white as they blend together,
Black-tip tails woven into the grain,
Twined in one continuous slither—
A moment of summer that will remain.

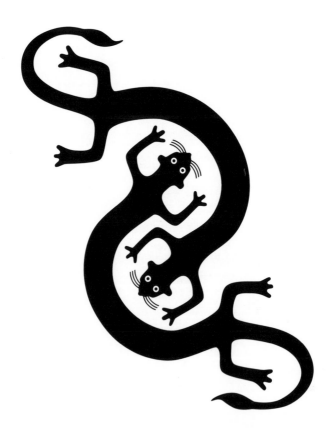

Traditional Gifts

Something old, beautiful, and dead;
Something new, that's filled with dread;
Something borrowed, that must be repaid;
Something blue, that will slowly fade.

My youth is old, beautiful, and dead;
My age is new, and filled with dread;
My life is borrowed, and must be repaid
Into the blue, and slowly fade.

O youth, grow old without the dread,
And age, retain a young head;
May life not always take away
And blue skies fill the borrowed day.

The Pigeon's A to Z of London

You may have heard the rumour of the great
  Bloomsbury bloomer,
Or the filled baguette bonanzas of Earl's Court's
  extravaganzas;
But to earn your daily bread, and ensure that
  you're well fed,
It's *The Pigeon's A to Z* that will guarantee
  street cred.

Bits of Finsbury Park paratha make a quite
  delicious starter,
And there's good Swiss Cottage loaves you can
  polish off in droves.
For your wholemeal—wheat and oat—you'll
  find Hampstead is afloat,
And anywhere that's posh offers croissants
  and brioches.

Puri at Hounslow East is a veritable feast,
And in Petty France you can (sometimes) pick up
  petit pains;
But should your sights be fixed on a delight—
  dough bread in Brixton
Can be tempting for your dinner, as is teacake
  out at Pinner.

Try a Clapham Common bench for a crusty
      stick of french,
Or go north to Golders Green where the bagels
      must be seen;
There is often bread and quark on the lawns
      of Belsize Park
(If the hedgehogs haven't had it, or
      the cats, after dark).

There are waffles all with topping down
      in fashionable Wapping,
And along the Kilburn High Road, a scofa
      bread or soda;
While a football match at Wembley makes a
      pigeon go all trembly
At the thought of all the tons of discarded
      burger buns.

The pitta's always pleasant around
      Mornington Crescent,
And, although the flight is longer, they do finger
      rolls in Ongar;
If you find you're in Whitechapel, a chapati
      or a bap'll
Fill a gap till you can fly away to Peckham
      for some rye.

The naan will give a mouthful if you're out
    as far as Southall,
And if you're up for looting, we propose the
    toast at Tooting;
While in Fulham you can scratch a decent
    meal from focaccia
And in Islington they scatter bits of
    olive-baked ciabatta.

The pumpernickel's good in Finchley
    Road and Cricklewood,
And the Temple Fortune chollah gets you hot
    under the collar.
Crumpet's always on the go if you linger
    in Soho,
But *if* you want a nice tip—try the granary
    in Ruislip.

From the bake-your-own in Catford to the
    sandwiches of Stratford,
A pigeon in the city's clearly sitting very pretty.
With the crumbs of London Town, be they
    black or white or brown,
A pigeon isn't prejudiced—for he'll eat any
    bread you list.

On the Move

When lions have had enough of your talk,
They stalk.

When mice realize they have to hurry,
They scurry.

When camels have really got the hump,
They slump.

When kestrels on hover are ready to swoop,
They stoop.

When bulls in a china shop are at large,
They charge.

When foxes sit in the shadows and sulk,
They skulk.

When snakes feel they're all of a dither,
They slither.

When hens are grubbing around on spec,
They peck.

When spiders don't want to do any work,
They lurk.

When wasps decide to have a fling,
They sting.

When cows wake from post-prandial slumber,
They lumber.

When sheep are in their quiet phase,
They graze.

When kangaroos go off in a flounce,
They bounce.

But when we are in for a long walk,
We baulk.
We shamble and shuffle,
And scramble and scuffle,
And kick up a rumpus and dust—
For we'll only move if we must!

The Winter's Tale
(in memoriam Dorcas 1988–97)

Imagine a cat with big yellow-green eyes
And silky fur, grey-tabby and white.
Imagine she's 'rescued' one autumn night.
The cat is dead. Long live the cat.

Imagine a cat who nuzzles your chin
And cuddles your neck with each soft paw,
A cat who couldn't love you more.
The cat is dead. Long live the cat.

Imagine a cat who gets travel sick
And has to be given a calming pill.
Imagine that cat on the window sill.
The cat is dead. Long live the cat.

Imagine a cat who likes to hunt mice
And brings them in when they're still alive.
You save them, hoping they will survive.
The cat is dead. Long live the cat.

Imagine this cat, when you've gone to bed,
With her head on the pillow next to you
And one arm clasping your shoulder too.
This cat is dead. Long live the cat.

Imagine a road where no stars shine
And darkness shrouds the grassy bank.
Draw the cat's cradle as one small blank.
The cat is dead. Long live the cat.

Winter has hit with a bang and a whimper;
A car caught Dorcas out too late.
Now, Mopsa must grow to her sister's estate.
The cat is dead. Long live the cat.

Canon

The wheel of Chance spins and turns.
Where will it stop? Nobody knows,
Nobody learns.

Where will it stop? Nobody knows.
Nobody learns where luck's to be found—
It comes and goes.

Nobody learns where luck's to be found.
It comes and goes like a wayward breeze
Without a sound.

It comes and goes like a wayward breeze,
Without a sound or backward glance,
As fate decrees;

Without a sound or backward glance,
As fate decrees whose numbers top
The wheel of Chance.

As fate decrees whose number's top,
The wheel of Chance spins and turns.
Where will it stop?

The wheel of Chance spins and turns.
Where will it stop? Nobody knows.
Nobody learns.

Growing Older

Yet another autumn's here—
The drear nights are drawing darkly in,
And evening lights
Come on
To kill the day.
Still, life's too short to waste thoughts
On mortality every blessèd year!

Three Rounds

Cat's cradle, cat's cradle,
With string we are able
To crisscross our fingers
And tie them in knots.

* * *

I've searched the garden three times over
Looking for a four-leaved clover.
If at last I do discover
One, I'll give it to my lover.

* * *

Sing a song of serendipity,
Black cat creeping in the long green grass;
Luck can't bring you true serenity—
Let it pass, let it pass.

Full Eclipse April 1996

It started with a fraying at the edge,
The merest hint of black around the arc
That slowly, minute-slowly slid a wedge
Across the moon's white circle in the dark.

The merest hint of black around the arc,
Earth threw its shadow up against the night
Across the moon's white circle in the dark,
Was in no hurry, savouring each bite.

Earth threw its shadow up against the night,
Sidling its way over the pale round—
Was in no hurry, savouring each bite.
The moon eclipsed, it gave way to our ground

Sidling its way over the pale round.
Strange to think our shadows were there too.
The moon eclipsed, it gave way to our ground
Which swallowed hard, then lingering withdrew.

Strange to think our shadows were there too
That slowly, minute-slowly slid a wedge
Which swallowed hard, then lingering withdrew.
It finished with a fraying at the edge.

Macho Man at the Beach

Little terns are nesting
High up in the dunes,
Likely lads are resting
Listening to tunes;
Sonia is divesting
Clothes and solitude,
For she is quite arresting
Sunbathing in the nude.

Much too interesting
For lads to let go by,
They dream they are molesting
And giving her the eye.
Their horseplay turns to jesting,
They dare one to draw near,
But Sonia is protesting
So he runs away in fear

And goes back to contesting
The properties of beer.

Bully for Me

I'd love to be a fly on the wall,
Just to be present at your downfall.
Your peace of mind won't be worth tuppence,
Sooner or later you'll get your comeuppance.
Somebody somewhere will call your bluff,
It's not for me, enough's enough.
You're skating on ice that is ever thinner.
Meanwhile, I'd lay my eggs in your dinner.

It's No Picnic

If you eat out on the beach today
You're in for a big surprise;
If you eat out on the beach today
You'd better beware of flies;
For every wasp that ever there was
Will pass the word for certain because
Today's the day we're going to have our picnic.

Picnic time just isn't fun—
We can't sit down upon the ground before
    they're buzzing around!
Horseflies, thrips, and ladybirds,
And bumble bees who've heard where we
    can be found;
Why is our family singled out?
What makes them land upon my sandwich
    as contraband?
Every insect below the treeline
Will set its course and make a beeline
For us, because we're going to have a picnic!

The Cemetery Cat

It was a typically cold day
When we went to bury Uncle Fred.
Snow lay thick on the ground of the dead.

The cars crawled to the door of the church
And we shuffled into its whispering space.
Snow seemed to follow us into the place.

'I am the resurrection and the life'—
The coffin's procession was dignified.
I thought of Uncle Fred inside.

The organ played and we tried to sing
But the chill had laid our voices low.
Then something warm came out of the snow.

Singing along with loud miaows,
A ginger cat slipped in to pay
Respects to Uncle Fred that day.

It rubbed itself on the coffin's edge
And sniffed the flowers on the lid,
Listened, and sang, whenever we did;

Then followed us out to the open grave
And sat as we bowed our heads to pray.
What the vicar thought, I cannot say.

'Ashes to ashes, dust to dust.'
'Amen,' we said. 'Miaow,' said the cat.
Uncle Fred would have liked that.

Snapshots from a Childhood

(for Ann)

On warm summer days
We climbed our back garden fence
And ran down the path.

Then I'd lie cocooned
In cornfields, flat on my back,
Listening to larks

Whose songs high above
Filled the air with silver flutes
And made me feel free.

We buried treasure,
A box of coloured buttons,
In the river bank.

We would stalk strangers
Through the pines, indian-style,
On silent needles,

Or slide on bottoms
Down the steep, dry dusty slopes
Of the Valley's dell.

The 'seven sisters'
Clump of trees was where we launched
Our breakneck races.

Nearby we took turns
To chip away the chalk seam
And hollow a cave.

I still remember
The nutty taste of beech mast
Prised from angled shells,

And sweet nectar sucked
From clover petal tips, plucked
Like tiny pink quills.

True Confessions

I've *never* dived for pearls in coral seas,
I've *never* combed gorillas for their fleas,
I've *never* ever surfed on a southerly breeze,
And I've *never* tried to swing on a flying trapeze.
But—
I *have* collected honey from a hive of bees,
And I have to admit that I *have* talked to trees,
I have sometimes even succumbed to jealousies,
And I *have* made occasional enemies.

I've *never* found a pirate's treasure chest,
And I've *never* tried to climb Mount Everest,
I've *never* shot an albatross through its breast,
And I've *never*, yet, been under police arrest.
But—
I *have* been under surveillance in Bucharest,
And I *once* robbed a bird of an egg from her nest,
I've learnt that things can turn out for the best,
But I've been on several marches to protest.

I've *never* tried to fish in a mackerel sky,
I've *never* sung a frog a lullaby,
I've *never* been in court to testify,
And I've *never* seen the truth with the naked eye.
But—
I *have* flapped my arms in the hope I would fly,
And I *have* thoughtlessly made some people cry,
I *have*—sometimes—told a terrible lie,
And I've actually seen somebody close to me die.

* * *

There are things I'll never do, it's the same
old song,
There are things I still could, if they're not
left too long;
There are things I have done which were
just plain wrong,
And things that happened to me and
have made me strong.

Drat!

Our fat cat is a champion ratter
And it really doesn't matter what we say:
She commits assault and battery
Upon the local rattery,
Dispatches all her catches
And then fetches in the wretches
With a clatter through the catflap every day,
Where she leaves them on the carpet on display.

The Hedgehog

Tonight I listened to a hedgehog feed
As it shuffled close to the hedgerow's edge
With a deep low chunter of a rhythmic sound
Like the muted chug of an outboard motor.

It snuffled and snooped with its probing snout
As it sniffed and rooted under the leaves,
And every so often it smacked its lips,
Sucking and slurping on something juicy.

American Space Invader

You must remember this,
A kiss can go amiss,
You'll find this as you grow;
And even though you're only six,
You have to know.

Spontaneous affection
Is viewed as insurrection
Among the toddler ranks;
The PC lobby goes to war,
Calls out the tanks.

The social worker pounces,
The teacher then denounces,
And you're sent home from school.
The girl is given counselling.
It's just not cool.

We used to take our chances
With amorous advances,
And thrill to the kiss chase.
We look back with nostalgia to
The slap in the face.

But now it's come to this.
A simple friendly kiss
Will land you in disgrace.
So, boys, I wouldn't risk it. Don't
Invade her space.

On a Persian Satrap

Satraps
Don't wear flatcaps,
Ask for cashback,
Fit their own catflaps;
For Satraps
Have their slave chaps
For that.

Satraps
Issue diktats
On the backs of
Autocratic rulers;
Satraps
Govern whole tracts
Of maps.

Satraps
Should be fat chaps
Who set mantraps
To catch rats who lapse.
Detractors,
Ipso facto,
Collapse.

Smart chaps
Do not backchat
To a Satrap,
Crack a joke or backslap.
The rack is
Just a handclap
Away.

Lap cats
Like to catnap
On the flat lap
Of a Persian Satrap.
Satraps
Like their lapcats
To purr.

Satraps
Love their lapcats,
For a Satrap
Brooks no backchat claptrap.
Lapcats
Just take catnaps
And purr.

If you should
Meet a Satrap
With a lapcat
And a hidden trapdoor,
The safe track's
Not to wisecrack—
Stand back!

Murphy's Luck

Some people talk of Providence,
And some of smiling gods,
While others say Dame Fortune
With favour on them nods;
Some count on Guardian Angels
To help them beat the odds—
But all that ever works for me's
The law that's known as Sod's.

Two for the Lilywhite Boys

Tilly and Lily were terrible twins,
As like as two peas in a pod;
But Tilly was silly and lived willynilly,
And Lily was just plain odd.

Tilly and Lily, unfortunate girls,
Often dreamt of the day they would wed;
And so did their dad, with his hair turning grey,
'Who will rid me of them!' he said.

For Tilly and Lily were ugly, you see,
And nobody liked them as such.
'We'll just have to take things in hand,' they said,
'Or we'll never amount to much.'

So they went to the make-over make-up man
And emerged with brand new faces,
New clothes, new hair, and a new attitude,
And bulging in all the right places.

They swept the Lilywhite boys off their feet—
They'd never seen beauty so fair.
Billy for Tilly and Willy for Lily,
They married them then and there.

Now Tilly and Lily are Lilywhite wives,
With Lilywhite kids on the way;
But if ever the make-over make-up man tells,
There's sure to be hell to pay.

Face to Face

When I was young what frightened me
Was not the dark,
Was not the shadows on the wall,
Was not the night enclosing all,
Was not the park
Where strangers hid behind each tree.

When I was young what frightened me
Was on the pier—
The Laughing Sailor in his case
With wheezing laugh and sinister face
And sideways leer.
A penny bought this jollity.

Or was my mirror image where
My own eyes
Would stare me back and take control.
I seemed to see inside my soul
The hidden lies,
And like a stranger laid them bare.

But now what frightens me the most?
It is the dark,
It is the shadows on the wall,
The night that must enclose us all;
It is the stark
Stranger hidden behind each ghost.

Kyrielle

Dead leaves are on the steps again,
I tread on their fragility.
Another year clogs up the drain.
O, God of silence, let me be.

An owl is hooting in the Square—
The voice of our mortality.
The church is closed and no one's there.
O, God of silence, let me be.

There is a grave some miles from here,
A double home for family;
Dead leaves the only souvenir.
O, God of silence, let me be.

Don't tread upon the dead leaves of
The child I was, who's still with me.
Wind and time will make their move.
O, God of silence, let me be.